D1450189

FAR-OUT and UNUSUAL

pets

Poison Dart Frogs

Cool Pets!

Enslow Elementary
an imprint of

E | **Enslow Publishers, Inc.**
40 Industrial Road
Box 398
Berkeley Heights, NJ 07922
USA

http://www.enslow.com

Alvin and Virginia
Silverstein and Laura
Silverstein Nunn

Enslow Elementary, an imprint of Enslow Publishers, Inc.

Enslow Elementary® is a registered trademark of Enslow Publishers, Inc.

Library of Congress Cataloging-in-Publication Data
Silverstein, Alvin.
  Poison dart frogs : cool pets! / Alvin Silverstein, Virginia Silverstein and Laura Silverstein Nunn.
    p. cm. — (Far-out and unusual pets)
  Includes index.
  Summary: "Provides basic information about poison dart frogs and keeping them as pets"—Provided
by publisher.
  ISBN 978-0-7660-3881-3
  1. Frogs as pets—Juvenile literature. 2. Dendrobatidae—Juvenile literature. I. Silverstein, Virginia
B. II. Nunn, Laura Silverstein. III. Title.
  SF459.F83S55 2011
  639.3'789—dc22
                        2010054003
Future editions:
Paperback ISBN 978-1-4644-0126-8
ePUB ISBN 978-1-4645-1033-5
PDF ISBN 978-1-4646-1033-2

Printed in China
012012 Leo Paper Group, Heshan City, Guangdong, China
10 9 8 7 6 5 4 3 2 1

To Our Readers: We have done our best to make sure all Internet Addresses in this book were
active and appropriate when we went to press. However, the author and the publisher have no
control over and assume no liability for the material available on those Internet sites or on other Web
sites they may link to. Any comments or suggestions can be sent by e-mail to comments@enslow.com
or to the address on the back cover.

Photo Credits: © 1999 Artville, LLC, p. 7 (map); Age fotostock/Photolibrary, p. 35; AP Images/
Rob Carr, p. 23; Dante Fenolio/Photo Researchers, Inc., p. 13; © John Noltner Photography,
p. 43; Kate Baylor/National Geographic, p. 31; Mark Moffett/Minden Pictures, pp. 4, 7, 18;
Peter Arnold Images/Photolibrary, p. 39; © Robert Smith/Photobiologist.com, pp. 27, 32;
Shutterstock.com, pp. 3, 11, 15, 16, 21, 44; © Steve Greer/SteveGreerPhotography.com, p. 29;
Thomas Marent/Minden Pictures, p. 37; Wildlife/Photolibrary, p. 41.

Illustration Credits: © 2011 Gerald Kelley (www.geraldkelley.com)

Cover Photo: Shutterstock.com

Contents

Poison dart frogs come in a rainbow of colors!

1

Cool Colors!

Just one look at a poison dart frog, and wow!
You can't believe your eyes. This is no ordinary
frog. It is not a dull green or brown like you might
find in your backyard. Poison dart frogs come in
amazingly bright colors and patterns. They are
the wildest colors you have ever seen—yellow,
orange, red, and even blue! How cool would it
be to keep one as a pet?

But isn't it dangerous to have poison dart
frogs as pets? After all, their name does have the
word "poison" in it. In the wild, these frogs *are*
poisonous. That's because they eat insects that

feed on poisonous plants. This doesn't harm the frog at all. But the poisons can be deadly to any animal that tries to eat the frog.

Poison dart frog pets are actually harmless, though. They don't live on the same diet as they would in the wild. So their bodies don't have the dangerous poisons that their wild relatives do.

Poison dart frogs can make great pets. But keeping one is more like keeping a fish than it is like keeping a cat or dog, or even a hamster. These frogs are more for show than they are for cuddling.

Poison dart frogs can add beauty to any home, but they are also a big responsibility. These frogs need special care. How much do you know about these little beauties? Find out as much as you can before you bring one into your life.

Read on to see why poison dart frogs can make such far-out and unusual pets.

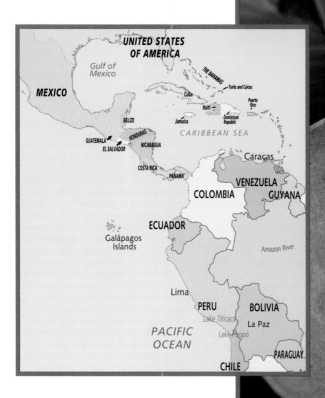

This man rubs a dart along the skin of a golden poison dart frog.

Far Out!

What's in a Name?

How did poison dart frogs get their name? One very poisonous kind lives in Colombia. The Choco Indians who live there use the frog's poisons for hunting. They coat darts by rubbing them along the frog's back. When the poisonous dart strikes its target, the poison seeps into the animal's body. In no time, the animal is unable to move.

2

Wild About Poison Dart Frogs

In the wild, poison dart frogs are easy to spot. Who could miss a bright blue-spotted frog sitting on a green leaf? Shouldn't it be hiding somewhere so it won't get gobbled up by a swooping bird? Like all frogs, poison dart frogs need to protect themselves from predators. Predators are animals that catch and eat other animals.

Actually, the frog's beautiful colors are like a warning sign that screams: "Don't eat me or else!" Enemies quickly learn to stay away from bright-colored frogs. Any animal that doesn't listen to the

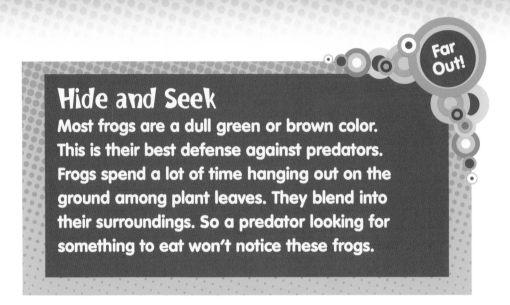

Hide and Seek

Most frogs are a dull green or brown color. This is their best defense against predators. Frogs spend a lot of time hanging out on the ground among plant leaves. They blend into their surroundings. So a predator looking for something to eat won't notice these frogs.

warning will get a mouth full of yuck! These frogs taste awful. A predator that eats one can get very sick or even die.

As pets, poison dart frogs don't have to worry about predators. But even in your home, they still keep their wild ways. Learning about how they behave in the wild can help you take care of this unusual pet in your home.

Life in the Wild

In the wild, poison dart frogs live in tropical places. The tropics are usually warm all year round. They are also rather damp. Poison dart frogs can be

In the wild, poison dart frogs can be found in trees. They also live among leaves, logs, and rocks on the forest floor. This is a harlequin poison dart frog.

found in the rain forests of Costa Rica, Colombia, Peru, Bolivia, and Venezuela. They live on the Hawaiian Islands as well. They tend to hang out in trees, near puddles, and among the leaves, logs, and rocks on the forest floor.

Like all frogs, poison dart frogs are amphibians. *Amphibian* comes from a Greek word that means "double life." Frogs do have a kind of double life. They can live on land and in the water, just as other amphibians do. This also describes their two life stages: a fishlike tadpole (the young form of frogs) and an adult. (Adult frogs start out small and continue to grow for many months.)

Tadpoles grow from frog eggs. They live completely underwater. When they become adult frogs, they spend most of their time on land. But water is still important to them. Their smooth, slimy skin needs to stay slightly wet. Frogs have lungs to breathe, like we do. But they can breathe through their moist skin as well. They also drink water by taking it in through their skin.

After the eggs hatch, a male poison dart frog carries the tadpoles to the water. This male tricolor poison dart frog has tadpoles on his back.

How does a frog stay wet when it no longer lives in the water? In the rain forest, the air is filled with tiny bits of water. The amount of water in the air is called humidity. Rain forests are very humid. That means there's a lot of water in the air. That's good for the poison dart frogs. The humid air keeps their skin slightly wet.

Skin Snot?

Ever wonder why a frog's skin feels so slimy? That's because the frog's skin is covered with mucus. That's like the stuff inside your nose that forms snot! It may be yucky, but it's useful. In your nose, mucus traps dirt to keep it from getting into your body. On a frog's skin, mucus helps hold in the wetness from the humid air.

Poison Dart Frogs Up Close

Poison dart frogs are not big fat frogs like the ones you might see hopping in your backyard. Most are only 1 to 2 inches (25 to 51 mm) long. Some are so tiny they are called "thumbnail frogs." (They are smaller than an adult person's thumbnail!) They are usually about ½ to 1 inch (13 to 25 mm) in size.

Poison dart frogs have some of the most striking colors and patterns. They come in bright shades of red, orange, yellow, green, and blue. Some have combinations of colors, with patterns of spots, bands, or splotches. One interesting type is called

Some poison dart frogs have bold bands of colors!

A blue jeans frog looks like it is wearing denim jeans.

the "blue jeans frog." It has a bright red or orange body with blue legs. It looks like it's wearing a pair of denim blue jeans on all four of its legs!

You Are What You Eat

Poison dart frogs are not the only poisonous frogs. In fact, many frogs have some poison in their bodies. But poison dart frogs are not born poisonous. They start out their lives completely harmless—and helpless against predators. The poisons they are so famous for actually come from eating poisonous insects. These tropical insects

Poisonous or Not?

Not all brightly colored frogs are poisonous. Some colorful frogs trick predators into thinking they're the poisonous ones—when really they are not. They may be able to avoid being eaten by animals that have learned to stay away from colorful frogs.

Far Out!

The golden dart frog is the most poisonous of the dart frogs.

become poisonous by eating poisonous plants. The poisons do not harm the insects or the dart frogs. The poisons quickly build up in the frogs' skin. The more insects they eat, the more poisonous they become. Some dart frogs are more poisonous than others.

There are more than two hundred kinds of poison dart frogs. Only three kinds are deadly to people. In fact, one of these super-poisonous frogs, the golden poison dart frog, has enough poison to kill ten grown men. Another name for this bright yellow frog is the "terrible poison dart frog."

Actually, the poison dart frogs raised by people are harmless. They don't eat poisonous insects, so no poisons build up in their skin. Even wild frogs lose their stored poison when they are caught and kept on a nonpoisonous diet. But the poison dart frogs sold as pets today are not taken from the wild. They are hatched and raised by pet breeders.

3

A Home for Your Frog

So you want a poison dart frog? Where do you get one? Don't worry—you don't have to travel to the tropics to find one. Many people breed poison dart frogs in America and in other parts of the world. You don't have to live in a really warm place to keep these tropical pets. But you do have to set up the frog's new home as close as possible to its living conditions in nature.

Probably the best place to get your own poison dart frog is from a breeder. Breeders usually take special care of their animals. They have raised

These dart frogs are so small, five of them fit easily
in this person's hand.

Do Pet Stores Sell Poison Dart Frogs?

Some pet stores sell poison dart frogs. But a pet store is not a good place to get one. Workers may not know much about these tropical animals. In fact, they may not even know whether or not their frogs were taken from the wild. If they were, the frogs could still be poisonous. It takes a while for the poison to leave the frog's body. So make sure to get your poison dart frog from people who know a lot about the frogs they are selling.

these frogs from the moment they hatched as tadpoles. These frogs are not poisonous at all. They don't eat the same poisonous insect diet they would have in the wild.

Breeders can give you information on a frog's background. They can also answer any questions you might have.

Should you get more than one poison dart frog? Young frogs (under six months of age) usually get

It is best to buy your pet dart frog from a breeder. This breeder is holding a golden poison dart frog.

along with one another. You can have several of them together without a problem.

As adults, however, many dart frogs become territorial. In the wild, their territory is the area where they live and get their food. They may fight each other over feeding areas and breeding spots. Males may fight other males to win over a female. Some females may fight, too.

Handle With Care

"Look, but don't touch!" That's good advice when it comes to poison dart frogs. Even as pets, you shouldn't pick them up. That's not because they are poisonous. It's because you could hurt *them*. They may get stressed out. They may squirm around in your hands. You could accidentally hold the frog too hard and crush a leg. The frog might even try to leap out of your hands.

If you do need to handle your poison dart frog, be very gentle. Even if there are no poisons, touching the frog's skin could still be harmful. Frogs may carry a type of bacteria called salmonella. It can spread to people and make them sick. It is best to wash your hands after handling your pet.

When two dart frogs fight, it is quite a sight. They may wrestle or chase each other around. Sometimes a frog will leap on another's back. The little attacker will then try to show who's boss.

When a poison dart frog is raised as a pet, it will think of the tank as its territory. If you want to avoid problems between frogs, just stick with one. But if you do get more than one, you could keep them in a big tank. Placing rocks and other objects in the tank as "hideouts" might also help. If fighting becomes a problem, though, you might have to remove the troublemaker and put it in a separate tank.

All the Comforts of Home

A 15- to 30-gallon tank is a good size home for up to four adult poison dart frogs. The bigger the tank, the better—especially if you plan on keeping several frogs together. They need room to roam around. The tank should be tightly covered with a mesh lid.

Cover the bottom of the tank with aquarium pebbles. Put down a layer of mesh. This helps to drain any extra water. Then add a layer of soil and peat moss. (You can plant live tropical plants in the soil and peat moss mixture.) On top of this, scatter around some branches, leaves, and tree bark. Also, make sure to include objects such as rocks that the frog can climb on or hide under.

Be sure to keep the tank in a warm place. Remember, poison dart frogs are from the tropics. They do well in temperatures between 75°F and 78°F (24°C and 25°C). But don't let the tank get too warm. In the wild, poison dart frogs spend a lot of time on the ground, where it is cooler.

Mist the tank a few times a day. This will keep your frog's home moist.

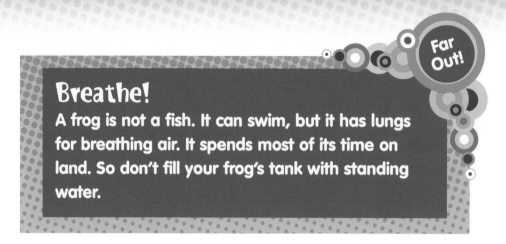

Breathe!

A frog is not a fish. It can swim, but it has lungs for breathing air. It spends most of its time on land. So don't fill your frog's tank with standing water.

If they get overheated, their skin could dry out. So keep the tank out of direct sunlight. You can use a thermometer inside the tank to make sure the temperature is just right.

How do you keep your frogs warm? You can place a heating pad underneath the tank. Pet shops sell tank heaters that would also work. Lights high up in the tank can give both light and heat. Fluorescent lights give enough light without making the tank too hot. Be sure to get the temperature just right *before* you put the frogs in the tank.

It is a good idea to keep the lights on a timer. They should shut off at night. Remember, you are trying to make your pet's home like the dart frog's

The frog's tank needs to be warm. Lights and a thermometer help control the temperature.

natural home. In the tropics, it gets dark and a little cooler when the sun goes down. At night, it is all right to let the temperature drop down to the 60s (degrees Fahrenheit).

Humidity is also very important. The frog's home needs to be damp. Use a spray bottle to mist the tank two to three times every day. But you do not need to make it *wet*. If the tank dries out too

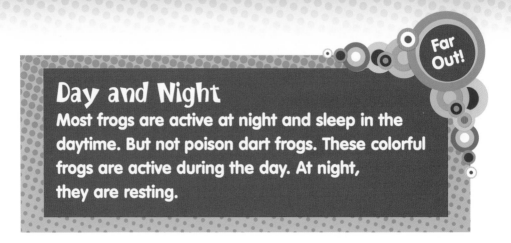

Day and Night

Most frogs are active at night and sleep in the daytime. But not poison dart frogs. These colorful frogs are active during the day. At night, they are resting.

quickly, you can put some pieces of solid Plexiglass over parts of the mesh top. (This will help hold in the moisture.) A shallow bowl of water that the frog can climb into and out of can help it keep its skin moist.

Feeding Time!

Poison dart frogs get very active when it comes to feeding time. This could be a good time to watch them. Why? Because they like to eat their food while it's still alive!

Poison dart frogs are small animals, so they need to eat tiny food. Live crickets are one of the most popular foods to give these frogs. But the feeder crickets you might find in a pet store are too

These frogs are being fed fruit flies.

big for them to eat. (Their mouths are too small.)
Poison dart frogs *can* eat newly hatched crickets,
called pinhead crickets. These young crickets are
less than a week old. You probably won't find them
in a pet store. It is better to get them from a
feeder insect company.

Wingless fruit flies are another good food
for your frogs. They are easy to raise yourself.
They are also cheaper than buying crickets.
You can buy wingless fruit flies from a local pet
store or pet supply company. (Make sure to get

You can grow your own wingless fruit flies. It is a good idea to keep them in a container like the one shown here.

Poison dart frogs eat pinhead crickets. These crickets are newly hatched and are tiny enough to fit in the poison dart frog's small mouth.

Grow Your Own!

Wingless fruit flies are a great food for poison dart frogs. But since they are so tiny, dart frogs need to eat a lot of them. An adult poison dart frog can eat more than fifty wingless fruit flies a day. You can save a lot of money if you grow your own at home.

Start with a few fruit flies. Put them in a jar with a mixture of mashed bananas and oatmeal. Cover the jar with a paper towel, held on with a rubber band. Within a few days, you'll have hundreds of fruit flies in the jar. The fruit flies don't actually eat the oatmeal and bananas. They feed on tiny bacteria that grow on the rotting fruit.

the wingless kind. Otherwise you'll have them flying all over the house.)

Poison dart frogs can eat a variety of other bugs as well. These may include springtails and Phoenix worms. You can buy any of these from feeder insect companies.

You don't need to worry about giving your dart frogs a water dish. As long as the inside of the tank is humid, the frogs can "drink" in the wetness through their skin.

4

Raising Your Frogs

You can't teach a poison dart frog to do tricks. And you can't take one for a walk or cuddle up with it on the couch. But that doesn't mean these colorful creatures don't make cool pets. Their snazzy-looking colors are only part of the story.

What could be more interesting than an animal that leads a double life? Frogs are famous for going through metamorphosis. This is a seemingly magical change that happens as an animal grows from a youngster into an adult. Frogs start life as fishlike, plant-eating creatures. They live in the water. Eventually, they turn into completely

These frogs are getting ready to become someone's pets.

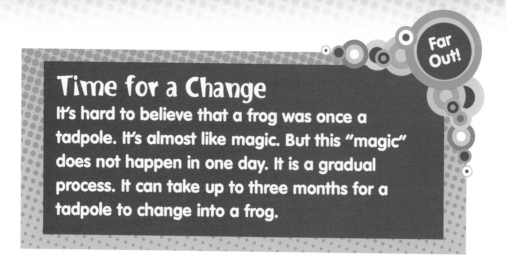

Time for a Change

It's hard to believe that a frog was once a tadpole. It's almost like magic. But this "magic" does not happen in one day. It is a gradual process. It can take up to three months for a tadpole to change into a frog.

different animals, ones that hop around and eat bugs. As adults, they live on land. If you keep male and female dart frogs together, you may be able to see the stages of metamorphosis with your own eyes.

A Frog's Life

What happens when frogs go through the change called metamorphosis? When frogs hatch from eggs, they don't look at all like their parents. The baby frogs are wriggling, fishlike creatures. They have big, round heads and long, flat tails. At this stage, they are called tadpoles.

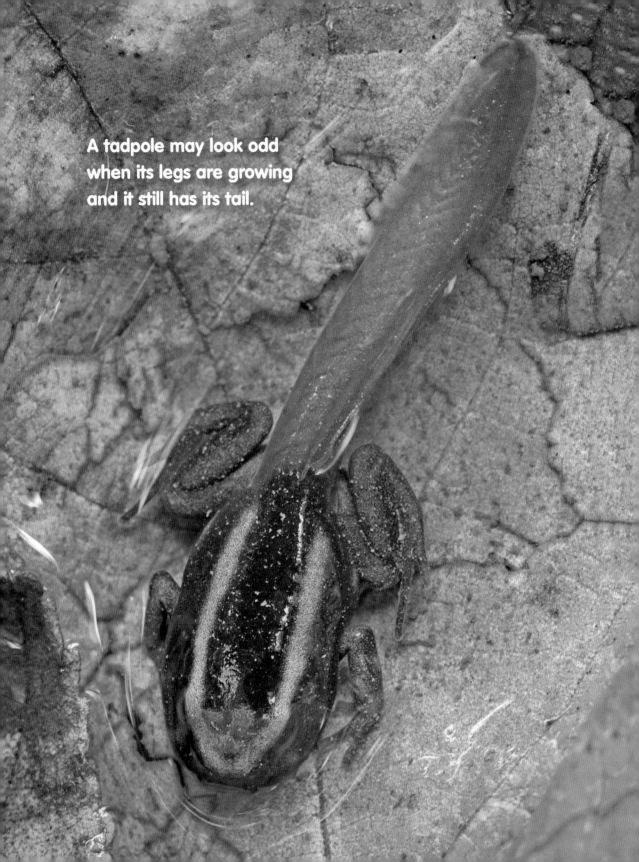

A tadpole may look odd when its legs are growing and it still has its tail.

For a long while, the little tadpoles just swim about in the water. They feed on small bits of green plant life and grow larger and larger. They do not have lungs for breathing air. Instead, tadpoles breathe through gills on the sides of their heads, just as fish do.

As a tadpole starts to change, two little knobs, or buds, appear near the back of its head. There's one on each side, close to where the head joins the tail. Each day, the buds grow larger. Soon they begin to look like legs. At first, they are short and stubby, then longer with webbed toes. These are the back legs. The tadpole looks a little odd at this stage. It has a big head, a tail, and a pair of long back legs, but no front legs. Then in a week or two, two more buds appear, farther forward. Within days, they grow into perfectly formed front legs.

The little tadpole is looking more and more like a frog. Interesting changes are going on inside its body, too. It is growing a pair of lungs so that it

A female dart frog is larger than the male.

Male or Female?

How can you tell the difference between male dart frogs and females? Generally, females are bigger and have a wider body. Some male dart frogs have wide fingers and wider toe pads. The females have long, skinny fingers with narrow toe pads.

Far Out!

can breathe air. Its gills start to disappear. Teeth are growing in its mouth. A tadpole can eat green plants that grow in the water. But as a frog, it will not eat plants at all. It will feed on insects and other animals.

For a time, the froglet is in a kind of in-between stage. It is no longer a tadpole, but it is not yet a frog. It can no longer live on plants. But it is not yet able to catch its own food. And so the tadpole stops eating. It doesn't starve, though. It lives on its tail! The frog's body absorbs the tail and uses it for energy. Each day the tail gets shorter. At last it disappears. Finally, the change is complete.

Raising Tadpoles at Home

You may see some signs that a frog couple is ready to mate. A female may chase a male she is interested in. If the male is interested, too, he may call to her from time to time. They continue to follow each other around the tank until the female finds a place to lay her eggs.

Frog eggs need to stay damp.

You can provide a place for the frog to lay her eggs. It can be a margarine lid or some other container lid. The breeding spot needs to be damp. Hide it behind a rock or some other object for privacy. Remove the dish of eggs from the tank after they are laid. (Otherwise the adult frogs may eat them!) Replace the dish with a clean one in case the frog lays more eggs.

Put the eggs in a clear plastic container. Add enough water to keep the eggs slightly wet, but not flooded. Don't let the eggs dry out. Use a spray bottle to keep them moist.

When the tadpoles hatch, put them in a container of water. It is best to move them to separate cups. If you put them all together in a

Too Many Frogs?

Poison dart frogs don't lay as many eggs as other frogs. Most lay up to ten at a time. And not all of them survive. Still, if you are lucky enough to breed frogs successfully, what do you do with all of them?

You may need to find your new frogs a new home. Perhaps your friends will take some. Or you can give them to a zoo. Maybe your school will be willing to take some as class pets. You don't want to let the dart frogs loose in the neighborhood. Unless you live in the tropics, chances are these frogs will not survive. And if they do, they may cause problems for other wildlife.

Poison dart frogs can make wonderful pets.

tank, they may eat each other. Change the water a couple of times a week. Feed the tadpoles small amounts of flake fish food or commercial tadpole food every day.

When the back legs develop, put objects such as rocks and branches into the water. That way the frogs can climb out of the water when their front legs develop. At this point, make sure the container has a lid because the frogs will be able to climb up the sides of the tank.

When the frogs have all four legs and their tails are almost gone, remove them from the water. They can drown, so make sure to check on them every day. You will need to put them in a new tank.

Before you started reading this book, did you wonder how people could keep a pet with the word "poison" in its name? By now you know that dart frogs aren't poisonous at all—as pets. These beautiful frogs are a real joy to watch. And their dazzling colors can brighten up any home.

Words to Know

amphibian (am FIHB eee un)—A type of animal than can live in the water and on land.

gills—Organs for breathing underwater.

humidity—The amount of water in the air.

metamorphosis (meh tuh MOR fuh sis)—A major change in an animal's form as it grows and develops.

predator—An animal that catches and eats other animals.

salmonella (sal muhn NEL uh)—A kind of bacterium (germ) that makes people sick. It may be spread by touching reptiles or amphibians and then touching the mouth or food.

tadpole—The young form of a frog or toad; it has gills for breathing, a tail, and no legs.

territory—The area where an animal lives and gets its food. Some animals will defend their home territory against others of their own kind.

Learn More

Books

Bartlett, R.D. *Poison Dart Frogs*. Hauppage, N.Y.:
    Barron's Educational Series, Inc., 2003.

Kingston, Anna. *The Life Cycle of a Poison Dart Frog*.
    New York: Gareth Stevens Publishing, 2011.

Moffett, Mark. *Face to Face with Frogs*. Washington,
    D.C.: National Geographic Children's Books, 2010.

Sihler, Amanda, and Greg Sihler. *Poison Dart Frogs*.
    Neptune City, N.J.: T.F.H. Publications, Inc., 2007.

Web Sites

Poison Dart Frogs—Info and Games

<http://www.sheppardsoftware.com/content/animals/
animals/amphibians/poisondartfrog_f.htm>

National Geographic. Photo Gallery: Poison Dart Frogs

<http://animals.nationalgeographic.com/animals/
photos/poison-dart-frogs/>

Index